seasalt
COLORING BOOK

Make your own mark on this collection of iconic
designs from the Seasalt archive. This book
contains 80 original illustrations and patterns
created by our small team in Cornwall, UK.
They're totally unique, you won't find
them anywhere else!

seasalt
COLORING BOOK

For artists of all ages

80 DESIGNS BY SEASALT ARTISTS

RYLAND PETERS & SMALL
LONDON • NEW YORK

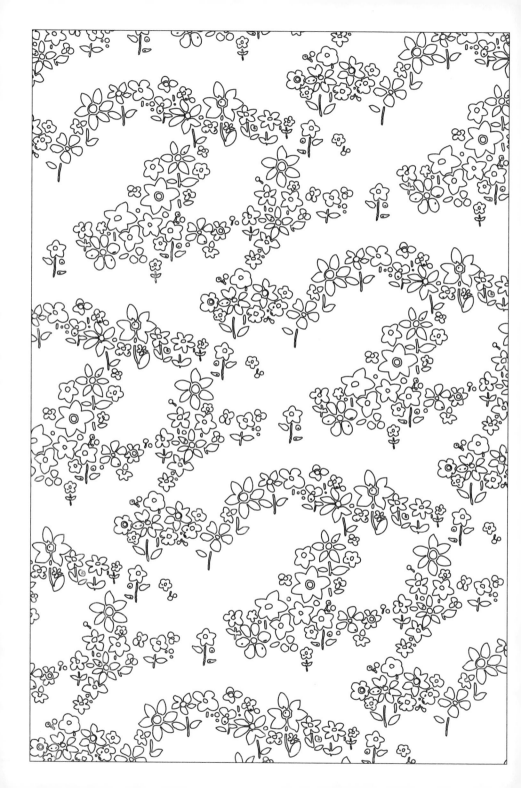

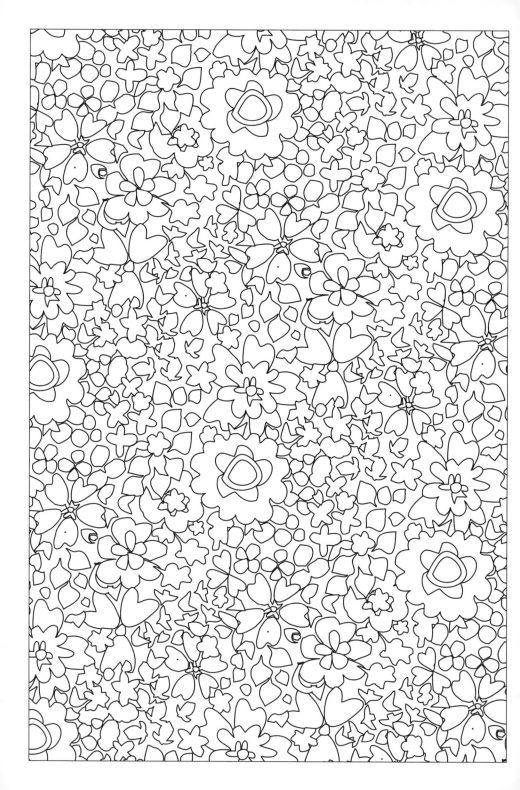

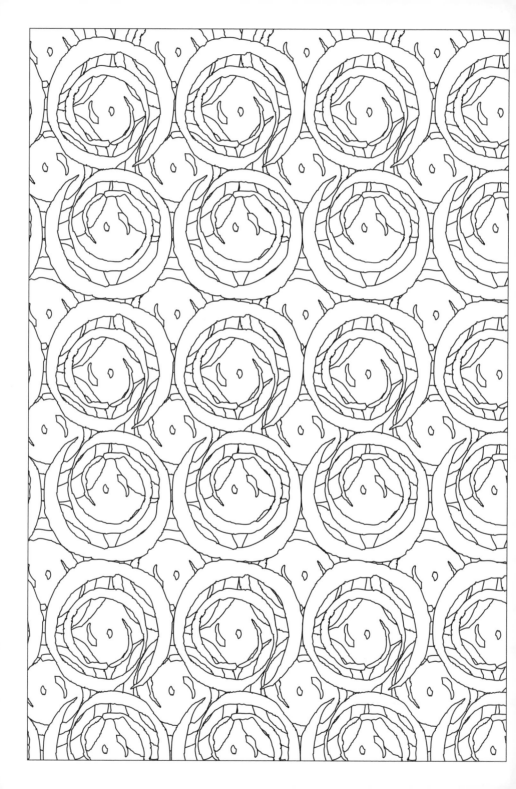

seasalt

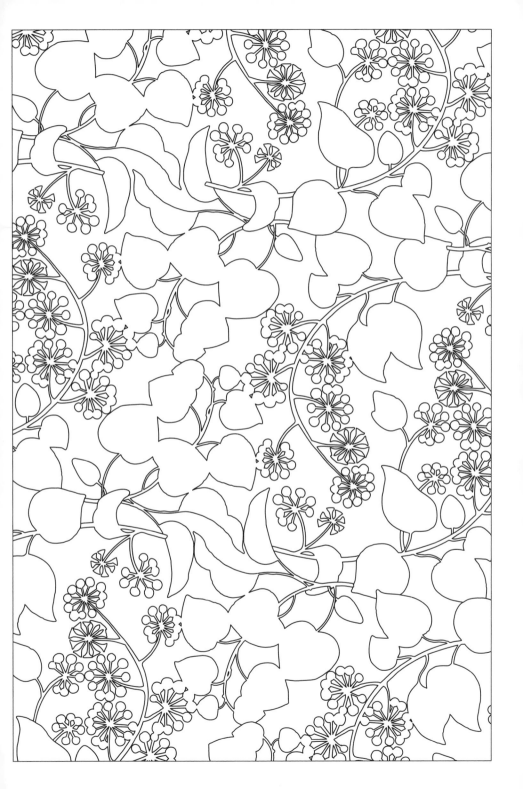

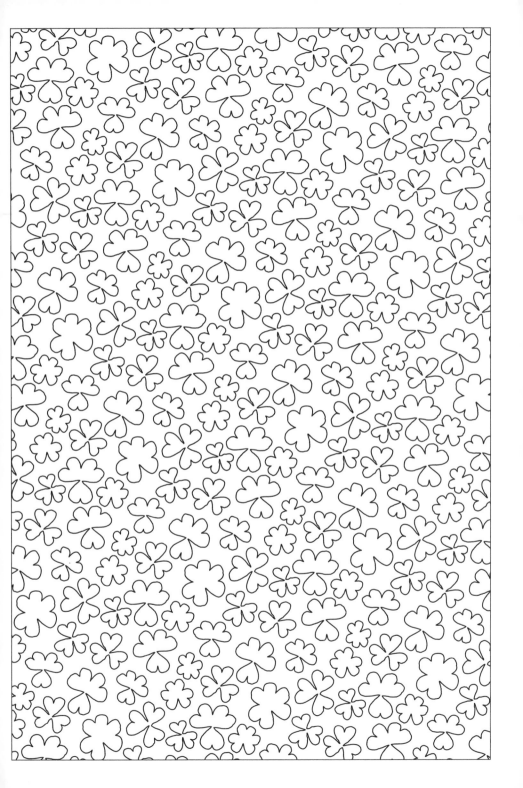

DESIGNER *Elly Jahnz*
COMMISSIONING EDITOR *Stephanie Milner*
HEAD OF PRODUCTION *Patricia Harrington*
ART DIRECTOR *Leslie Harrington*
EDITORIAL DIRECTOR *Julia Charles*
PUBLISHER *Cindy Richards*

FIRST PUBLISHED IN 2016 BY
RYLAND PETERS & SMALL
20-21 JOCKEY'S FIELDS
LONDON WC1R 4BW
and
341 E 116TH ST
NEW YORK NY 10029

UNDER LICENSE FROM SEASALT LIMITED.
seasalt **IS THE ® TRADE MARK OF SEASALT LIMITED.**

WWW.RYLANDPETERS.COM
WWW.SEASALTCORNWALL.CO.UK

ILLUSTRATIONS BY *Sophie Chadwick, Sara Bassett,*
Emma Kerswell, Matt Johnson, Elly Jahnz,
Wina You, Jacqui Winter & Jennifer Armitage.

UK ISBN (Seasalt Colouring Book): 978-1-84975-745-4
US ISBN (Seasalt Coloring Book): 978-1-84975-746-1

10 9 8 7 6 5 4 3 2 1

A CIP record for this book is available from the British Library.

US Library of Congress CIP data has been applied for.

Printed and bound in China